CONTENTS

Foreword by U.S. Representative Sarah McBride . . *vii*

Note to Our Readers . . . . *xiii*

A Reaffirmation of American Principles . . . . *xvi*

I. In America the Law Is King 1

II. List of Grievances 13

III. Thoughts on Constitutional Government . . . 21

IV. Thoughts on Liberty 55

V. To Secure the Blessings of Liberty and Equality 69

Activists' Resources *82*

About the Authors *86*

THOMAS PAINE

Portrait by George Romney, engraving by William Sharp, 1793

COMMON SENSE

IN THE AGE OF TRUMP

A Guide to Keeping Our Republic

RONALD K.L. COLLINS
RUSSELL W. HUXTABLE
AMY L. MARASCO
PAUL M. SPARROW

TOP FIVE BOOKS
OAK PARK, ILLINOIS

A TOP FIVE BOOK

Published by Top Five Books, LLC
521 Home Avenue, Oak Park, Illinois 60304
www.topfivebooks.com

Library of Congress Cataloging-in-Publication data available upon request

ISBN 978-1-938938-83-2 (paperback)
ISBN 978-1-938938-84-9 (ebook)

Cover & book design by Top Five Books
Printed in the United States of America

The cause of America is in a great measure the cause of all mankind....

Men who look upon themselves born to reign, and others to obey, soon grow insolent; selected from the rest of mankind their minds are early poisoned by importance; and the world they act in differs so materially from the world at large, that they have but little opportunity of knowing its true interests, and when they succeed to the government are frequently the most ignorant and unfit of any throughout the dominions....

[I]n America THE LAW IS KING. For as in absolute governments the King is law, so in free countries the law *ought* to be king; and there ought to be no other....

—Thomas Paine
Common Sense (1776)

There is no need to eulogize Thomas Paine. His life-long devotion to the cause of freedom; his undaunted, unshrinking advocacy of truth; his deep-seated hatred of kingly and priestly despotism, are his best eulogies. He was the architect of his own monument ... a monument that will last as long as the memory of a man.... But to honor the memory of Thomas Paine ... we must endeavor to carry out what he so nobly began, for his principles were not for one age or nation, but for all.

—Ernestine Rose
suffragist, abolitionist, and freethinker (1852)

FOREWORD

by

U.S. Representative Sarah McBride

COMMON SENSE by Thomas Paine has shaped the American story for centuries. One of the most influential pamphlets of its time, the central argument—that the colonies should declare themselves independent from the British crown—reflects a fundamental truth: building the America we know and love begins with believing in a country capable of fulfilling its promise and potential.

What *Common Sense in the Age of Trump* captures so urgently is the moment we are now in—as a country, as citizens, and as patriots. At the founding of our nation, we faced a crossroads, and we declared boldly that independence was the way forward. We did so with the hope of building a new nation. Today,

250 years after *Common Sense* circulated through the colonies—and as we mark 250 years after the founding of our nation—we find ourselves at a crossroads once again.

Throughout our nation's history, through the triumphs and the turmoil, we have borne witness to many great achievements—the American experiment chief among them. But the America we know and love is not self-sustaining. Each generation is called to defend it—and to continue to build it. As we face this choice again, we must ask ourselves: Do we capitulate to those who centralize power and erode our democratic norms? Or do we stand up, as generations before us have, and defend the country we love?

The beginnings of this nation were humble; a country built on the hopes and dreams of those who came to these shores in pursuit of freedom. Freedom of speech. Freedom of religion. Freedom from tyranny. Freedom from fear. Now, two-and-a-half centuries later, those very freedoms are being stripped away in more ways than we ever thought possible through executive orders, court decisions, and blatant disregard for precedent and the rule of law.

What we are living through right now is an era of corruption, when some in power would rather align themselves with billionaires, authoritarian leaders, and wannabe dictators than strengthen our democratic institutions. We are living through a moment when division and fear are stoked for political gain. A moment when decisions of enormous consequence are made without clarity, accountability, or care for their human cost. And yet, in the face of all this, people across the country continue to show up—organizing, speaking out, and engaging in what the late Congressman John Lewis called "good trouble."

I know your advocacy may not always feel like enough, and there may be moments when you feel powerless. But if you can take comfort in anything, take comfort in this: I have seen change firsthand. I have seen progress that once felt unimaginable. I am certain that our founders could never have envisioned someone like me writing these words today or serving our nation in the way that I do.

The way I see it, our democracy can only endure if we maintain hope—and faith in one another's capacity for growth and change.

Now we must decide whether we truly believe in democracy. Not as a talking point. Not as an abstraction. Not only when it benefits us or feels easy. But whether we genuinely believe it is worth defending. And whether we are willing to continue defending it.

As we commemorate the 250th anniversary of this nation's founding, I believe we have two-and-a-half centuries of evidence that show us how progress is possible. How we can restore faith in our government. How we can rebuild trust in one another. How we can strengthen our democracy.

The authors of this book are my friends, my colleagues, and my allies—but most importantly, they are builders of hope. They believe, as I do, that we have a shared responsibility to improve our nation for the generations that follow us. They make a powerful case for continued civic engagement—not withdrawal from it—and for using every tool at our disposal.

But hope isn't just a slogan or a sentiment; it's a democratic necessity—and is an active ingredient in citizenship. Because citizenship is not always easy, and hope does not always come naturally. It must be chosen, nurtured, and defended—built.

At every other defining moment in our history, when our bonds have been tested, we have faced the same fundamental question: do we destroy, or do we build? Do we abandon our Union, our Constitution, and our democracy? Or do we continue the work of building a more perfect one?

These moments come in cycles, and, as the living memory of past crises fades, we risk repeating them. When the memory of the American Revolution dimmed, we faced a Civil War. When the memory of the Civil War faded amid the Great Depression, some called for authoritarian leadership modeled after the strongmen of Europe. And now, as we lose the last members of the Greatest Generation, we again see voices seeking to undermine our democracy.

We live in an age in which cynicism is easy and corrosive. It erodes our faith in the very systems meant to empower us. Those who wish to destroy our systems thrive on cynicism—and they exploit it.

—They seek to dismantle government and strip it for parts.
—They weaken access to essentials such as housing and health care to consolidate power.
—They destabilize economic opportunity and leave working people to pay the price.
—They fracture our sense of shared purpose so that we turn against one another.
—And, aided by algorithms and authoritarians alike, they seek to convince us that democracy itself cannot deliver.

Now, eighty-one years after World War II, as its lessons fade from living memory, we are once again at a crossroads—and we are faced with a defining choice for our Union, our Constitution, and our democracy.

Will we *destroy*—or will we *build*?

As we mark 250 years since our founding and reflect on the endurance of this nation, I believe the answer is clear. We can and must continue building, sustained by hope. Because to lose hope is to abandon our duty—to our country, to the ideals of our founding, and to one another.

There's no denying that these are difficult times. But the path forward remains within our reach: to believe in our country, to believe in our Constitution, to believe in our neighbors and the communities they strengthen—and, above all, to believe in the power of hope.

Because in moments like these, hope is not naïve. It is common sense.

We're in this together.

U.S. Representative Sarah McBride
Delaware's At-large Congressional District
May 2026

NOTE TO OUR READERS

THE four of us, proud citizens of Delaware (the first state to ratify the Constitution), share our thoughts with our fellow Americans. We do this out of concern for our beloved nation. Marking the 250th anniversary of our independence, it is a fitting time to reflect on the troubling state of our country. We look to our history and the hopes of our founders for guidance and inspiration. We find renewed faith in the works of two great patriots: Thomas Paine's *Common Sense* and the Declaration of Independence by Thomas Jefferson. We reaffirm the great principles of freedom that these two patriots established in 1776. Then, as now, "these are the times that try men's [and women's] souls." A "decent respect to the opinions of humankind requires" us to speak out. Prudence, indeed, calls for us to do so.

The authoritarian actions of the Trump presidency demand that now, as in 1776, we stand up to express our disdain for tyranny, our contempt for demagoguery, and our scorn for a government steeped in falsehoods and slanders. We fear, and with due cause, that the state of affairs in our nation is reaching a tipping point, a point at which the very pillars of our democratic republic are under unbridled attack, and could collapse if left unchallenged. The despair and division of the moment are rampant. Hence, the need to redress our grievances in the hope that a spark might ignite in the minds and souls of our fellow Americans: now is the time to end such despotism.

In the words of Paine, penned on December 19, 1776: "Tyranny, like hell, it's not easily conquered; yet we have this consolation with us, that the harder the conflict, the more glorious the triumph." To be sure, this is not the time for the "summer soldier," the "sunshine patriot," or the silent citizen. The repeated "injuries and usurpations" of power, so prevalent today, invite "the establishment of an absolute Tyranny."

Jefferson's admonition bids us to wake up and take united action to oppose the authoritarianism that threatens to destroy all that we Americans hold dear.

Tracking Tom Paine's approach in *Common Sense*, we offer our case in the first four chapters, then outline our call to action in the final chapter. The hope is that our words will empower those opposed to Trump's antidemocratic actions. For those unsure what to think, we hope they can be swayed. For those who have supported the president, we hope they will be stirred to reconsider some of their views, mindful of the principles bequeathed to us by our founders.

Discourse, after all, underscores the uniqueness of our republic; freedom of speech and press define us and set us apart, and have always been the tools we use to adjust and open our minds.

Despotism is the cancer that breeds division and spreads hate; our forebears united to oppose it. It is this all-powerful authoritarianism that we once again confront with common sense and wise measures, for the love of our country, all the people living in it, and future generations—so they can enjoy its journey and strive to build a more perfect Union.

Take heed: in this crisis, those who shrink from the genuine service of our country pave the way for the very tyranny that rallied our founders to rebel.

Let the word go out: those who stand strong now, who express their opposition in words and deeds, deserve the love and thanks of every American.

Lewes, Delaware
May 2026

A REAFFIRMATION OF

WHEN in the course of human events it becomes necessary for a people to reaffirm the principles upon which their government rests, and to insist that power be exercised only with the consent of the governed; a decent respect to the opinions of humankind requires that they should declare the causes that impel them to this reaffirmation.

We hold these truths to be fundamental: that all persons are created equal; that they are endowed with certain inherent rights, including life, liberty, equality, and the pursuit of happiness; that governments are established to secure these rights, deriving their just powers from the consent of the governed; and that whenever any form of government becomes destructive of these ends, it is the people's right to call it to account and demand its correction.

AMERICAN PRINCIPLES

Prudence dictates that long-established governments should not be challenged for light and transient causes; and accordingly, experience has shown that people are more willing to suffer while evils are tolerable than to insist on reform. But when a long series of abuses and usurpations shows a deliberate intent to concentrate power at the expense of liberty, it is the right—if not the duty—of *we the people* to speak plainly and to restore constitutional balance to our beloved republic.

As the late Supreme Court Justice Louis Brandeis once reminded us: "Those who won our independence by revolution were not cowards. They did not fear political change. They did not exalt order at the cost of liberty." That wise advice remains as relevant today as it was nearly a century ago.

I

IN AMERICA THE LAW IS KING

The illusion that fooled all saved none.
—Albert Camus

WE do not invoke Camus to predict America's downfall. Not while there's still something we can do about it. Instead, we believe that all of us are once again at a critical juncture—one where attentive and fair-minded Americans need to pause, step back, and evaluate our current state and direction. Every culture must confront its excesses; each must contest its injustices; and everyone needs to reaffirm those core values without which no government can claim legitimacy. How the present unfolds into the future largely depends on how *we the people* act at these pivotal moments that shape our destiny.

We are at a turning point. Illusions, fear, and corruption heavily shape life in our nation today. Everywhere you turn, division is fueled by falsehoods and malice. Time and again, this destructive blaze is stoked by reckless actions that negate America's principles. Sadly, there seems to be no limit to how far the ruling party will go to ensure that no other party can ever again claim even a share of that rule.

This is our country; these are our times. Superficiality, lies, greed, and lawless executive actions define the moment. A destructive cynicism clouds our view of life, while many fail to see the threat of totalitarian control. Self-serving narratives replace truth from those sworn to safeguard our democracy, and are echoed in media outlets aligned with their interests. Lies abound of tales of the "enemy within"; of protesters really being paid actors, or "domestic terrorists"; of nonwhite immigrants coming to engage in crime, steal our jobs, and "replace" us; of the election that was "stolen" and the terrible wrongs committed against this president by the "unhinged radical left." The amount of disinformation is intended to dishearten as much as it is to mislead—so that, even if you don't believe the obvious lies, they have the effect of engendering a sense of helplessness and cynicism. Once this cynical mindset infects our lives, its destructive stain spreads everywhere.

Why? How did things come to this? Let us go back in time to set the framework for answering such questions. To do so, we return to *Common Sense* and remind our fellow Americans of what Paine wrote to pave the path for America's founding. Think of what he said to the colonial patriots to rekindle the spark of liberty in their heads and hearts:

> But where, say some, is the King of America? I'll tell you, friend, he reigns above, and doth not make havoc of mankind like the Royal Brute of Great Britain. Yet that we may not appear to be defective even in earthly honours, let a day be solemnly set apart for proclaiming the Charter; let it be brought forth placed on the Divine Law, the Word of God; let a crown be placed thereon, by which the world may know, that so far as we approve of monarchy, that in America THE LAW IS KING. For as in absolute governments the King is law, so in free countries the law *ought* to be king; and there ought to be no other.

Kingly power, that is the evil. And that power is fed by a quest for greatness, though not genuine greatness free of the taint of tyranny. Think of Donald Trump's recycled slogan, the one that captured the hearts (if not the minds) of so many, namely, "Make America Great Again." He first mouthed it on November 7, 2012, the day after President Obama was reelected. Ronald Reagan had used essentially the same phrase ("Let's Make America Great Again") as a slogan for his 1980 presidential run. In 2015, Trump adopted it for his 2016 presidential campaign and, with an acquisitiveness that knows no bounds, filed to trademark the phrase later that year. To further inflame his base, he also reveled in tagging his adversaries (especially his media critics) as "enemies of the state." But what did this appeal to "greatness" really mean? And how did his other vicious mantra figure into his agenda?

This obsession with "greatness" had less to do with America than with the image of himself and how he wanted that image to become widely accepted, now and in the future. The phrase also used imaginary perfection to suit a fictional past, one that was nevertheless popular with his political base. It was a *perfect* America, free of faults. Those who disputed that false portrayal of history were, following Stalin, branded "enemies of the people." In reality, the so-called greatness of which he spoke was bigoted, greedy, aggressive, unjust, and cruel.

Trump tapped into his vanity and used superlatives to portray his actions, intelligence, and so-called accomplishments. For example:

- "Nobody's bigger or better at the military than I am."
- "Nobody knows more about debt than I do."
- "Nobody knows more about trade than me."
- "Nobody knows politicians better than me."
- "Nobody has ever done so much in the first two years of a presidency as this administration."
- "My proudest legacy will be that of a peacemaker and unifier."

He described himself as a "very stable genius," and to the same end, he once called himself the "greatest communicator in the history of American politics." Trump persistently used self-promotion to create a "cult of personality," this to make *his* America more a nation ruled by its Supreme Leader than one governed by the rule of law and all that implies. By his measure, what matters is what is *perceived* rather than what is actually done. That perception has a transformative psychological power insofar as it trades the reality of a situation for the "reality" ordained by the Leader and imposed by his subordinates.

"Dictatorships survive," as Professor Jason Stanley reminds us, "on the myth that one single leader defines and embodies the nation. Fascism survives off myths that create an outgroup, who are relegated to second-class citizenship, at best." As the king is elevated, certain groups of people are denigrated or even prosecuted.

Of course, such claims to superiority and unmatched greatness are antithetical to limited government and to the constitutional government fashioned by our founders. A despot, intoxicated with his power, knows no limit, seeks no limit, and thereby acts as if his illusion of absolute power rendered him God-like. By Trump's reckoning, neither the laws of the land nor the laws of necessity constrain him. *More* is his mantra, *limit* is his nemesis.

Greatness grounded in such supreme images suggests that "the king can do no wrong." That mindset calls to mind something Trump said in 2016: "I could stand in the middle of Fifth Avenue and shoot somebody, and I wouldn't lose any voters, okay? It's, like, incredible." Then, in February 2025, Trump referred to himself as "King" and posted "Long live the King!" on social media. To add to the vanity and crassness, the White House posted a forged *Time* magazine cover on its X site featuring Trump wearing a crown. That brand of greatness smacks of the thinking of Caligula, ancient Rome's infamous ruler, who was a vain, sadistic, and mentally unstable tyrant. True to his demented character, his behavior was fanatical and erratic.

Greatness, when linked to political power as it often is, comes with a certain price even before the oppressive hand of tyranny appears. People must be duped time and again and by any means. As Hitler told a British reporter in June 1934: "At the risk of appearing to talk nonsense, I tell you that the National Socialist movement will go on for 1,000 years! . . . Don't forget how people laughed at me 15 years ago when I declared that I would one day lead Germany. They laugh now, just as foolishly, when I say I will stay in power!" That movement required time and propaganda to build; it involved appealing to the masses, even in the crudest forms.

To claim greatness in this way requires a strong-arm ruler. He must, like this president, have an entirely subservient cabinet; he must be able to control lawmakers through fear or submission; he must be able to summon the military to do his bidding at home and abroad; he must be able to rely on uninformed acquiescence from his followers; and he must be able to persecute and prosecute his opponents—those "enemies of the people."

Such counterfeit greatness must also foster a feigned crisis that demands extreme executive action. In a world where "enemies" lurk in every rival corner, *emergency* powers must become the norm. Extremist *exceptions* must become the rule. In the calamitous tumble of it all, there is no law, there is only the exceptional authority of a ruler whose emergency powers are unconstrained.

Trump's "greatness" also relies on a pattern of constant distractions. He doesn't care if it involves lying, as long as he avoids accountability. He doesn't mind making strange statements or taking outrageous actions. His main strategy is to distract until people become overwhelmed. In this game of diversions, he hides behind a curtain of evasiveness until he reemerges to praise his so-called achievements. When greatness is associated with lying in the service of unlimited executive power, constitutional constraints become meaningless; federalism loses significance; and individual rights are irrelevant in relation to fundamental notions of due process. Similarly, the concept of separation of powers becomes a farce whenever one branch (such as the executive branch) dominates. Moreover, the idea of justice based on fair laws becomes absurd when it is so easily bypassed or openly disregarded.

The "king can do no wrong" notion of greatness must maintain itself by fear, force, and illusion—here, the illusion "that fooled all and saved none." That illusion depends on:

- the corruption of language, of making the false argument seem true and vice versa;

- the devaluation of truth and the relentless repetition of propaganda;
- the demise of informed legislative policy owing to blind allegiance to the president; and
- an orchestrated effort to have a compelled and compliant media.

Be they towers, centers, institutes, an airport, or a train station, they all must display Trump's name—by his direction, of course, but always under the guise of being some administration lackey's idea. His image must also appear on coins and be draped on banners on government buildings. Time and again, he has proven that he is more interested in monuments to himself than in meaningful or lasting policy changes. He has also ordered that defamatory plaques be placed next to White House photos of any former president he dislikes. Likewise, his White House must be gaudy enough to match his kingly bent: it must be showy, with every inch of the formerly dignified "People's House" covered in gold trim. Then there is his proposed presidential library. According to NPR's Rachel Treisman, "President Trump has plans to splash his name across a sky-high presidential library in Florida.... [An] architectural rendering, [which he proudly showcased, depicted] a skyscraper towering over the rest of the Miami skyline, emblazoned with

Trump's last name and an American flag beneath a red, white, and blue spire. Inside—through a gold doorway bearing the presidential seal—military aircraft sit next to a golden escalator reminiscent of the one Trump rode down when he announced his first candidacy in 2015."

True to his twisted view of the presidency, he took a wrecking ball to the East Wing of the White House in the fall of 2025 without warning or approval from anyone else to make space for a $400 million, 90,000-square-foot ballroom—"one of the greatest ballrooms in the world." On March 31, 2026, however, U.S. District Judge Richard Leon ordered an immediate halt to the construction of Trump's lavish ballroom project. "The President of the United States is the steward of the White House for future generations of First Families. He is not," declared Judge Leon, "the owner."

Since the king "can do no wrong," he cannot make mistakes—others must always be held responsible for any of his failures or wrongdoings. Similarly, criticism of anything he does must be labeled as "fake news," regardless of its truthfulness. Contradictions must be ignored: what was openly stated yesterday can be blatantly denied tomorrow as if it never happened.

Trump's king-worshipping cult has no place in America. Its "greatness" is born of an illusion, a perilous one. Its "greatness" is rooted in vanity and vindictiveness. And its claim to supremacy is contrary to those founding values that truly allowed America to be great—that is, when its principles were faithfully honored as required by Article II, section 3 of the Constitution. The lesson: when "greatness" ceases to be honorable, it ceases to be constitutional.

II

LIST OF GRIEVANCES

The present state of America is truly alarming to every man who is capable of reflection.

—Thomas Paine
Common Sense (1776)

THE record of executive power exercised by the 47th president reveals a pattern of repeated wrongs and usurpations, all aimed at undermining democratic norms and centralizing authority. Furthermore, as each day passes, the situation worsens, with no clear end in sight. To illustrate Trump's abuses of power, let the following 28 grievances, among others, be presented to a "candid world," as Thomas Jefferson did in 1776:

1. **He has fomented rancor by fostering division rather than unity,** and by appealing to fear and grievance rather than to shared responsibility and the common good.
2. **He has applied the law not with equal justice, but with selective severity,** deploying immigration enforcement in ways that terrorize entire communities, separate families, and punish anyone who opposes it without due process of law.
3. **He has permitted and overseen the use of deadly force by federal agents against civilians,** including American citizens, during domestic enforcement actions, without sufficient transparency, accountability, or independent judicial review.
4. **He has escalated federal force within civilian communities,** introducing militarized agents into neighborhoods far removed from any declared emergency, provoking fear, unrest, and the loss of life rather than ensuring public safety.
5. **He has called forth armed forces within our borders,** placing National Guard units and federal troops on standby or into service in response to civilian peaceful protest, chilling the free exercise of speech and assembly.

6. **He has usurped Congress's lawmaking powers** and imposed his will on the people through unlawful and excessive executive orders.
7. **He has waged an undeclared and costly war** inconsistent with the objective of Article I, section 8, clause 11 of the U.S. Constitution.
8. **He has corrupted the Department of Justice** by making it subservient to his arbitrary wishes, ordering the prosecution of his political enemies, and granting clemency to those who have curried his favor.
9. **He has destroyed the structure and legitimate purpose of administrative agencies** to the detriment of the economy, the environment, public health, and the administration of justice.
10. **He has violated the Emoluments Clauses of the Constitution** by equating public service with personal gain, permitting grift to flourish in the shadow of authority, and he has used access and influence to enrich the few while corroding trust in the many.
11. **He has usurped the rights of the States** by coercing states and municipalities through threats and conditional funding rather than cooperation, partnership, and mutual respect.

12. **He has coerced universities and law firms** to comply with his ideological views, no matter how vengeful or purposeless they are.
13. **He has denied due process,** relying on illegitimate administrative authority and enforcement mechanisms that sidestep judicial oversight and erode constitutional protections against unreasonable searches, seizures, and detentions.
14. **He has abridged the First Amendment** by punishing people and the press for exercising their First Amendment rights.
15. **He has repeatedly lied to the American public** and has likewise demanded that those serving under him do likewise.
16. **He has denied equal justice to African Americans** by siding with white nationalists, weakening civil rights through unjust executive orders, and by discriminating against people of color in direct and indirect ways.
17. **He has cruelly denied the rights of LGBTQ+ people,** both civilians and those in the military, without providing due process.
18. **He has governed by unwarranted emergency decrees,** extending extraordinary powers into everyday use and normalizing what was meant to be rare and temporary.

19. **He has obstructed independent accountability,** resisting transparent investigation when federal actions result in injury or death, thereby undermining public trust in the rule of law.
20. **He has behaved as if his office made him above the law,** promoting the dangerous idea that election results justify executive wrongdoing and that power alone grants legitimacy—contrary to the fundamental principle of a republic that the law is supreme over all.
21. **He has abused his governmental powers to feed his vanity** by naming and renaming structures or designing events or currency in his self-image.
22. **He has encouraged the people to excuse what they would never tolerate in another,** demanding loyalty where accountability is owed, and dismissing lawful oversight as persecution rather than the ordinary function of self-government.
23. **He has fostered conflicts of interest and self-dealing,** weakening ethical norms not by repeal, but by neglect, and teaching by example that personal advantage may outweigh public duty.

24. **He has misused public resources under the banner of reform,** promoting initiatives that promise efficiency yet deliver waste, confusion, and abuse; substituting spectacle for stewardship.
25. **He has empowered unaccountable actors in the purported name of government efficiency,** allowing efforts such as the so-called "DOGE" work to proceed without adequate transparency, oversight, or measurable public benefit, thereby squandering public funds and undermining confidence in responsible governance.
26. **He has unlawfully used his power to impose** sweeping, arbitrary tariffs and economic measures that burden working families, farmers, and small businesses while bypassing meaningful legislative deliberation.
27. **He has mistaken the patience of the people for their consent,** relying upon fatigue, distraction, and division to shield misconduct from consequence.
28. **He has secretly awarded private companies no-bid government contracts** at inflated prices.

IN every stage of these abuses, the people have petitioned for redress in respectful and lawful terms. Too often, their petitions have been met with dismissal, delay, false replies, violent repression, and/or the repetition of the injury itself. A government whose character is thus marked cannot be the sole judge of the limits of its own authority.

We respectfully remind our fellow Americans that the Constitution is meant to limit government power, not to grant those in charge unchecked authority. We urge them to think carefully, be fair, and respect the laws that protect everyone. We also remind them that liberty, once surrendered in the name of authoritarian power, is rarely recovered without a high cost.

We therefore reaffirm that the exercise of power without limits invites tyranny; that securing allegiance through coercion is contrary to democratic principles; that political retribution conflicts with core principles of fairness; that free expression is threatened whenever the government silences critics; that authoritarian decrees cannot replace due process of law; that equality cannot coexist with privilege; that security should never come at the expense of justice; that presidential self-dealing undermines self-governance by the people; that enforcement without accountability is not law; and that no office—regardless of rank—can place its holder above the Constitution.

Guided by the principles of fairness and checks and balances entrusted to us by our forebears, *we the people* pledge not revolution, but vigilance; not disorder, but democratic engagement; not despair, but renewed commitment to the unfinished work of building a *more perfect Union*. We do this to strengthen the Union, to better establish justice, to ensure domestic tranquility, to provide for the common defense, to protect our environment, to promote the general welfare, and to secure the blessings of liberty and equality for ourselves and future generations.

III

THOUGHTS ON CONSTITUTIONAL GOVERNMENT

Tolerance becomes a crime when applied to evil.
—Thomas Mann (1924)

CONSTITUTIONAL government is a system with limited, delegated powers. Actions by government officials must be authorized by law and must comply with constitutional mandates. Powers should be divided among the branches, and rights must be protected. In all of this, the federal judiciary serves as the final authority on legal matters, subject only to constitutional amendments. This, at least, is the tradition of constitutional government in America. However, that tradition has been, and still is, under attack by President Trump and his administration, with the acquiescence and often enthusiastic support of his party's legislative branch members.

The Return of Kingly Rule

February 19, 2026. On that date, a long blue banner was draped on the exterior of the Justice Department's headquarters in Washington, D.C. It bore Trump's glowering image. It was yet another federal building supporting a streamer bearing the 47th president's face. Be it banners or buildings, the obvious message was always the same: all power must trace back to him; governmental authority begins and ends with him; law must be beholden to him; and a steady flow of emoluments must be directed toward him.

How did it happen that his exercise of executive powers vastly overshadowed those powers constitutionally assigned by the founders to the legislative branch? After all, the constitutional authority granted to the latter is more than twice that given to the president. The answers to such questions about this imbalance of power can be traced to two things:

First, to Trump's unparalleled and unlawful grasp of raw power.

Second, to congressional Republicans' abdication of their powers, out of fear of being savagely attacked by their president and, eventually, having to face a primary election opponent loudly endorsed by him.

Constitutional government in America was not, however, originally meant to be this way. More than anything else, the Constitution drafted in 1787 aimed to restrict executive power to prevent oligarchic rule. Paine stressed this point, Jefferson echoed it, and James Madison ensured it became the supreme law of the land. Yet, in reality, Trump has acted more like a king, as if there are no real checks on his authority. Viewed this way, kingly rule has returned to the very nation that once fought a bloody revolution to end such authoritarian power over its people.

On Tariffs and the Unauthorized Use of Executive Power

February 20, 2026: The Supreme Court, which up until then had been faithful to his wishes almost without fail, upset him greatly. Even two of his own nominees to the High Court defied him. The *tariffs* ruling infuriated him; it directly challenged the go-it-alone reach of his powers. In the words of Chief Justice John Roberts' majority opinion:

> The President asserts the extraordinary power to unilaterally impose tariffs of unlimited amount, duration, and scope. In light of the breadth, history, and constitutional context of that asserted authority, he must identify

> clear congressional authorization to exercise it [under the International Emergency Economic Powers Act.] IEEPA's grant of authority to "regulate . . . importation" falls short. IEEPA contains no reference to tariffs or duties. The Government points to no statute in which Congress used the word "regulate" to authorize taxation. And to date, no President has invoked IEEPA to confer such power. We claim no special competence in matters of economics or foreign affairs. We claim only, as we must, the limited role assigned to us by Article III of the Constitution. Fulfilling that role, we hold that IEEPA does not authorize the President to impose tariffs.

The Administration argued that the president's tariffs were legitimate and did not amount to an unconstitutional tax. The IEEPA law, it argued, authorized the president to impose tariffs of unlimited amount and duration on any product from any country. The Court correctly disagreed:

> Article I, Section 8, of the Constitution sets forth the powers of the Legislative Branch. The first Clause of that provision specifies that

> "The Congress shall have Power to lay and collect Taxes, Duties, Imposts and Excises." It is no accident that this power appears first. The power to tax was, Alexander Hamilton explained, "the most important of the authorities proposed to be conferred upon the Union." . . . It is both a "power to destroy". . . and a power "necessary to the existence and prosperity of a nation"—"the one great power upon which the whole national fabric is based."

The Chief Justice then added:

> The power to impose tariffs is "very clear[ly] ... a branch of the taxing power." *Gibbons v. Ogden* ... (1824). "A tariff," after all, "is a tax levied on imported goods and services." . . . And tariffs "raise[] revenue," . . . the defining feature of a tax. . . . Indeed, the Framers expected that the Government would for "a long time depend . . . chiefly on" tariffs for revenue. *The Federalist* No. 12, at 93 (A. Hamilton). Little wonder, then, that the First Congress's first exercise of its taxing power (and its second enacted law, right after the one providing for the new officials to take an oath) was a tariff law.

In his concurring opinion, Justice Neil Gorsuch lent staying power to Paine's words and Madison's concerns:

> Americans fought the Revolution in no small part because they believed that only their elected representatives (not the King, not even Parliament) possessed authority to tax them. Declaration of Independence ¶19. And, they believed, that held not just for direct taxes like those in the Stamp Act, but also for many duties on imports, like those found in the Sugar Act.

Americans later enshrined those beliefs in the Constitution. In other words, the president lacked the authority to impose tariffs as he did.

To be sure, Trump's rhetorical posturing was a bold attempt to undermine the legitimacy of a ruling that was both constitutionally sound and necessary. Nonetheless, true to form, the president demonized the justices who ruled against him. He called them "fools and lap dogs." He expressed disdain about some members of the Court, saying he was "ashamed of certain members of the court, absolutely ashamed for not having the courage to do what's right for our country." He declared their ruling a "disgrace to our nation" and described it as "deeply disappointing." But he was just getting started in his rambling press conference after the ruling, about which he bitterly complained. Ironically, he dismissed the ruling's actual impact on his powers. As his rage grew, he falsely claimed that the justices who ruled against him were influenced by "foreign interests." Regarding the two justices he appointed who voted against him, he tagged them "fools and lap dogs for the RINOs [Republicans in Name Only] and the radical left Democrats." He went further to say they were "very unpatriotic and disloyal to our Constitution." Meanwhile, his vice president, J.D. Vance, echoed predictable rhetorical loyalty: "This is lawlessness from the Court, plain and simple."

The 47th president's highly belligerent attitude symbolizes his kingly arrogance. He sees no limits on his powers; he has no respect for a system of checks and balances; he owes no allegiance to laws passed by Congress; and he considers it justifiable to go after anyone who dares interfere with his *supreme* will. To "make America great again" thus has little or nothing to do with the constitutional greatness envisioned by our founders, but rather with the *power* he can seize by breach or deceit.

Contrast that conviction with a basic tenet of our constitutional system: the president can only exercise power duly conferred upon him by the Constitution and/or by laws duly enacted by Congress. In other words, his discretion is not unbridled; his powers are not governed by his view of the law; and his duty to obey the rule of law cannot be abdicated simply because his complicit cabinet officers have lined up to defend his "right" to violate his constitutional oath.

When he exceeded his powers, that constitutional breach had consequences—specifically, a major economic impact. Because of the president's unlawful actions, the federal government was expected to owe an estimated $175 billion in refunds. These refunds, aimed at various parties, would cover tariffs illegally collected by the government. In 2025, administration lawyers told a federal trade court that the government would refund the tariffs if their collection was found unlawful. However, the president suspended that promise. Chaos was his justification: "It would take many years to figure out what number we are talking about and even, who, when, and where, to pay." He added, "It would be a complete mess, and almost impossible for our country to pay." As of May 2026, the matter remains in litigation limbo.

First, he acted unlawfully; then he vilified the Supreme Court for holding him accountable; and finally, he moved to stiff companies and Americans on the tariff refunds they were due.

Beyond the illegality of his actions, there is the economic reality of the tariff issue. In 2025 in the Rose Garden, he waxed on, assuring his audience that "jobs and factories will come roaring back into our country and you see it happening already." A year later, the truth was that all those promising jobs and factories hadn't appeared, at least not on the grand scale he predicted. More idle promises—his trademark.

Attacking Judicial Justice

Using the bully pulpit and social media, Trump has criticized judges who ruled against his unlawful actions. He called one federal judge a "most evil person"; he labeled another a "radical left lunatic"; he condemned jurists who questioned his authority as "communist radical left judges"; he lashed out at the "brazen defiance" of his will by federal judges who disrupted his illegitimate agendas. In an all-caps Memorial Day message on Truth Social, he condemned other judges who ruled against him in deportation cases, calling them "JUDGES WHO ARE ON A MISSION TO KEEP MURDERERS, DRUG DEALERS, RAPISTS, GANG MEMBERS, AND RELEASED PRISONERS FROM ALL OVER THE WORLD, IN OUR COUNTRY SO THEY CAN ROB, MURDERERS [*sic*], AND RAPE AGAIN, PROTECTED BY THESE USA HATING JUDGES WHO SUFFER FROM AN IDEOLOGY

THAT IS SICK." In the same post, he called the judges "MONSTERS" who want America "TO GO TO HELL." His then–deputy attorney general (and former personal defense lawyer) Todd Blanche described the campaign against disloyal judges as "a war." And his cabinet officials, along with others in his administration, have echoed his toxic assaults.

In a 2024 year-end report, Chief Justice John Roberts wrote: "Attempts to intimidate judges . . . are inappropriate and should be vigorously opposed." That admonition has been roundly ignored. The predictable result of Trump's demonizing has been a significant uptick in threats against judges who have had the temerity to rule against his unconstitutional programs. In 2025 alone, four hundred federal judges were targets of alarming threats. It represented a 78 percent jump in just four years. In a 2026 *60 Minutes* interview, Ron Zayas (the CEO of Ironwall, a company that scrubs judges' personal data from the web) noted that "in 14 years, he has never seen as many violent threats as today." Meanwhile, despite her characteristic bravado, his now former attorney general, Pam Bondi, remained dangerously silent on this issue.

On April 1, 2026, Trump attended oral arguments in the birthright citizenship case (*Trump v. Barbara*).

It was the first time a sitting president attended a Supreme Court case, never mind one specifically challenging a president's executive order. Perhaps it was yet another attempt to intimidate the justices and to ensure that his solicitor general, D. John Sauer, did not concede any points inconsistent with his wishes. When the Court signaled that it might actually rule against him during questioning, Trump, despite the clear command of the Fourteenth Amendment, called such constitutional compliance "stupid."

While the birthright citizenship and tariff cases suggest that Trump's broad powers could be checked by the Supreme Court, two points suggest otherwise. First, he has won the majority of cases brought before the Trump-friendly Court. Second, the Court's ruling in *Trump v. CASA* (2025) is highly relevant because it barred lower federal courts from issuing nationwide injunctions. In light of that, Professor Stephen Vladeck made a compelling point: in her separate opinion in *CASA*, "Justice Elena Kagan highlighted an alarming possibility: that the government would lose a bunch of cases brought by individual plaintiffs but never appeal its losses, so that it could continue to enforce a patently unlawful policy against anyone who didn't bring her or his own lawsuit to challenge it." In layperson's terms, as long as there is no Supreme Court ruling with a *nationwide* impact, Trump's unlawful orders will have to be challenged individually in 94 different federal district courts if his government lawyers decline to appeal unfavorable rulings.

When the tactical dust settled, it became clear that even the high court is not supreme when it comes to setting aside so many of Trump's unlawful orders. This was made possible by the Supreme Court in *Trump v. CASA* and the majority opinion authored by Justice Amy Coney Barrett, a Trump appointee.

The All-Powerful Supreme Executive

> *We have a president who can't handle the truth. . . . Tonight, we ask you to join us in choosing hope over fear, democracy over authoritarianism, the rule of law over lawlessness, ethics over unbridled corruption, resistance over complacency, unity over division, peace over war.*
>
> —Bruce Springsteen
> (Minneapolis, March 31, 2026)

A nation ruled by a political strongman is antithetical to everything for which our system of constitutional government stands. If any "unitary executive theory" of power tolerates (let alone invites) such rule, it does so at the expense of championing power over justice, of preferring unlimited powers to limited ones, and of favoring authoritarianism over democracy.

What we have observed since Trump took office in January 2025 is a government largely governed by executive orders, with little or no legitimacy. Its Justice Department has repeatedly and forcefully defended this unconstitutional power grab. The Department of Homeland Security (DHS) has used deadly force to assert its unchecked authority, and when challenged, has lied to courts and the American people. Then DHS Secretary Kristi Noem (with the White House press secretary's help) made wild, false claims. When federal judges ruled against the administration, the response was often to ignore those court orders. And whenever an agency official or government lawyer questioned the president's claim to unlimited power, they were quickly fired. The same goes for the press; any reporter who challenged his false claims or illegitimate power was fiercely condemned or even barred from government press briefings. In a well-functioning and constitutionally balanced democracy, serious policy questions should not be overwhelmed by precarious executive orders, though that has far too often happened.

All must march in ideological lockstep to his will.

Election Denial (or Challenging the Will of the People)

One of the pillars of democratic constitutional government is the finality of fair elections. Despite his numerous challenges and attacks on his political opponent, the Electoral College officially certified the results of the December 14, 2020, presidential election. Similarly, nearly every court that reviewed the issue of election fraud dismissed his "stolen election" claim for various reasons. In the summer of 2022, a comprehensive and well-documented report titled "Lost, Not Stolen" was produced by conservative judges (including former federal judges J. Michael Luttig and Michael McConnell), lawmakers (including former Senator John Danforth), and lawyers (including Theodore Olson). Here is what they said:

> We . . . have undertaken an examination of every claim of fraud and miscount put forward by [the] former President . . . and his advocates, and now put the results of those investigations before the American people, and especially before fellow conservatives who may be uncertain about what and whom to believe. Our conclusion is unequivocal: Joe Biden was the choice of a majority of the Electors, who themselves were the choice of

> the majority of voters in their states. Biden's victory is easily explained by a political landscape that was much different in 2020 than it was when [the] President... narrowly won the presidency in 2016. President Trump waged his campaign for re-election during a devastating worldwide pandemic that caused a severe downturn in the global economy. This, coupled with an electorate that included a small but statistically significant number willing to vote for other Republican candidates on the ballot but not for [the] President ... are the reasons his campaign fell short, not a fraudulent election.

To further emphasize their findings of no fraud, the conservative authors of the report added:

> [The president] and his supporters have *failed to present evidence of fraud* or inaccurate results significant enough to invalidate the results of the 2020 Presidential Election. We do not claim that election administration is perfect. Election fraud is a real thing; there are prosecutions in almost every election year, and no doubt some election fraud goes undetected. Nor do we disparage attempts to

> reduce fraud. States should continue to do what they can do to eliminate opportunities for election fraud and to punish it when it occurs. But *there is absolutely no evidence of fraud in the 2020 Presidential Election* on the magnitude necessary to shift the result in any state, let alone the nation as a whole. In fact, there was no fraud that changed the outcome in even a single precinct. It is wrong, and bad for our country, for people to propagate *baseless claims* that President Biden's election was not legitimate. (emphasis added)

And yet, Trump continues to claim that the results of the 2020 presidential election were fraudulent, and that the election was "stolen" from him—even though his former attorney general, William Barr, stated there was no evidence of significant election fraud. Nevertheless, the president pressured state officials to override the election results and appoint electors who would support him. At one point, Texas's attorney general, Ken Paxton, petitioned the Supreme Court. He sued the states of Georgia, Michigan, Wisconsin, and Pennsylvania, where certified results showed Joe Biden had won. The Texas AG alleged a variety of unconstitutional actions in the presidential balloting in those states—such arguments had already been routinely rejected by lower courts. The Supreme Court rejected the Texas challenge. Once again, the claim of election fraud was dismissed. But not by Trump, and not by anyone seeking his favor to this day.

The President of Peace?

In war, truth is the first casualty.

—attributed to Aeschylus

War Powers. Article I, Section 8, Clause 11 of the Constitution states that Congress shall have the power to "declare War, grant Letters of Marque and Reprisal, and make Rules concerning Captures on Land and Water . . ." Through its enumerated powers, Congress also has the authority to define and punish offenses against the law of nations; raise and support armies; establish and maintain a navy; make rules for the armed forces; provide for calling forth the Militia; and organize, arm, discipline, and govern the militia when in service of the United States. Additionally, Congress holds related powers, such as authority over appropriations and the Necessary and Proper Clause.

Heedlessly ignoring that constitutional mandate, the president has threatened or wielded war-like powers against Colombia, Cuba, Greenland, Iran, Iraq, Mexico, Nigeria, Somalia, Syria, Venezuela, and Yemen. In a major military action that risked a broader regional conflict, he ordered the bombing of Iran without any real or legitimate congressional approval. The February 2026 bombing of Tehran was carried out without any urgency, military or otherwise. And it was conducted at great public expense. Even in the early weeks of the war, the Pentagon sought more than $200 billion in a military budget request.

Shifting explanations. Trump provided one fabricated justification after another in an attempt to rationalize his war against Iran: 1) he attempted to justify the attack on Iran to destroy its nuclear bomb capabilities, despite previously praising himself for having "obliterated" its nuclear capabilities; 2) he falsely claimed that Iran was building missiles that "could soon reach the American homeland," and that he was taking military action to "eliminate imminent threats from the Iranian regime," though he provided no proof of that; 3) he tried to defend his actions by suggesting, against all odds, that the Iranian people could overthrow their government and the Revolutionary Guard; 4) when those reasons failed to persuade, his secretary of state, Marco Rubio, alleged that preemptive military strikes were necessary once Israel decided to attack Iran since U.S. "assets" might then be targeted; 5) although his administration claimed early on to have notified members of the Armed Service Committees in Congress, Democratic members of those committees were not informed; 6) his military actions also violated The War Powers Resolution of 1973 and the U.N. Charter, passed by the U.S. Senate and signed by President Truman in 1945, which prohibits the use of force "against the territorial integrity or political independence of any state"; 7) and though he initially denied that ground troops would be involved in the war, by late March 2026 the Pentagon said it was sending additional troops to the Middle East.

The Iran conflict was costly and unpopular and with no obvious endgame. With self-contradictory bravado, Trump described his actions as "foolish . . . but smart," and that he "would do it again."

"You've got to do it the right way," is how he put it in a March 2, 2026, statement to the press. His secretary of war (changed from "defense" at Trump's insistence), Pete Hegseth, provided his interpretation of what such statements meant when he proclaimed that the president need not abide by any "stupid rules of engagement." If such "stupid rules" (i.e., the Constitution, federal statutory law, and international law) did not bar military attacks on Iran, then by that logic, there would be nothing to prevent the president from taking military action (i.e., war) against Cuba or any other nation.

Beyond all that, there is the following irony: this was the *ninth* military operation of his second term. His drive, as he put it, "for large-scale military operations," was contrary to his MAGA mantra before all of that. As reported in the February 28, 2026, *New York Times*:

> When he first ran for president in 2016, Donald J. Trump disavowed the military adventurism of recent years, declaring that "regime change is a proven, absolute failure." He promised to "stop racing to topple foreign regimes." When Mr. Trump ran for president in 2024, he boasted of starting "no new wars . . ." The self-declared "president of PEACE" has chosen to become the president of war after all, unleashing the full power of the U.S. military on Iran with the explicit goal of toppling its government.

Furthermore, the irony is compounded when one considers what was also pointed out in the *New York Times* about what the president said before and after he was elected:

> **2012:** "Now that Obama's poll numbers are in a tailspin—watch for him to launch a strike in Libya or Iran. He is desperate."

> **2013:** "Remember that I predicted a long time ago that President Obama will attack Iran because of his inability to negotiate properly—not skilled!"

> **2016:** "We're going to stop the reckless and costly policy of regime change."

> **Election night 2024:** "I'm not going to start wars. I'm going to stop wars."

His vice president and cabinet members previously championed such sentiments. For example:

- In a 2023 *Wall Street Journal* op-ed, then Senator J.D. Vance wrote: "He has my support because I know he won't recklessly send Americans to fight wars overseas." He later ran as VP on a ticket branded "Pro Peace," at which time he declared: "Our interest very much is in not going to war with Iran. It would be a huge distraction of resources. It would be massively expensive for our country."
- Tulsi Gabbard, Trump's director of national intelligence, wrote on June 13, 2019, "Trump's shortsighted foreign policy is bringing us to the brink of war with Iran and allowing Iran

> to accelerate [its] nuclear program—just to please Saudis and Netanyahu. This is not America first." Later, she added, "We've got to stop Donald Trump from starting a war with Iran."

Despite the many wrongdoings by Iran's late supreme leader, Ayatollah Ali Khamenei, the decision to go to war went against what the president and his supporters had previously claimed. It also went against the powers granted to the people's representatives in Congress, the federal courts, and international law.

And, as with many of his actions, the specter of illicit profits looms in the background. In a March 24, 2026, article titled "Treason in the Futures Markets," Paul Krugman wrote: "People close to Trump are trading based on national secrets." The evidence? Some 15 minutes before Trump suddenly announced that the U.S. and Iran were in talks to end the war, causing a quick and isolated spike in trading volume in the S&P 500 and oil futures—this, according to MSNow, resulted in $1.5 billion in highly profitable and suspicious trading. The lesson: war, whether real or fabricated, can be profitable if only the surrounding messages are manipulated.

His Enemies List

The structure and content of the Constitution of 1788 and the Bill of Rights of 1791 aimed to define, and thus limit, the federal government's powers, protect the rights of the people, and maintain the powers reserved for the states. In principle, this reflected the realization of the ideals promoted in *Common Sense* and the Declaration of Independence. As before, those ideals are often undermined when a king or president exceeds their authority, especially for vindictive reasons. Once again, we see a disturbing rejection of those principles and a clear violation of constitutional laws.

The current Justice Department has opened investigations and pursued criminal cases against several of the president's political rivals and vocal critics. For instance, the U.S. attorney's office in Washington, D.C., aimed to have a grand jury indict six Democratic members of Congress who made a video advising members of the military that they could refuse to follow illegal orders. For doing so, the Justice Department sought to indict them for sedition. The members included Senators Elissa Slotkin and Mark Kelly, and Representatives Maggie Goodlander, Jason Crow, Chrissy Houlahan, and Chris DeLuzio. Following the law, a federal grand jury in D.C.

declined to issue any indictments. To continue their punitive efforts, Defense Secretary Hegseth appealed a federal court ruling that prevented him from punishing Senator Kelly, a former astronaut and retired captain in the U.S. Navy.

There was more, much more. For example, there were politically motivated actions taken against, among others, the following individuals:

- **James B. Comey** (former FBI director): At the president's urging, he was indicted twice by the DOJ. The first case was dismissed. As of May 2026, the second case was pending.
- **Letitia James** (New York Attorney General): Here again, at the president's urging, the DOJ sought to indict her for bank fraud and mortgage fraud criminally. A judge first dismissed the case, and a grand jury subsequently refused to indict her.

Several federal prosecutors and officials in the U.S. Attorney's Office were fired or resigned after they refused to charge Comey and James.

- **Don Lemon** (journalist): An outspoken critic of the president, he was indicted and arrested for conspiracy regarding a protest at a place of worship. He pleaded not guilty; he asserted he acted as a journalist, not a participant in disturbing a religious ceremony.

- **Tim Walz** (Minnesota governor) **& Jacob Frey** (Minneapolis mayor): Federal prosecutors served grand jury subpoenas to them as part of an investigation into whether they obstructed federal law enforcement in connection with an indiscriminate immigration campaign in the Minneapolis–Saint Paul area.
- **Chris Krebs & Miles Taylor** (former DHS officials): Both were targeted for openly criticizing the president and his administration.

Moreover, in January 2026, six federal prosecutors in Minnesota resigned after the Justice Department attempted to investigate the widow of Renee Good, the Minneapolis woman killed by an ICE agent, following the DOJ's failure to examine the legality of the agent's deadly shooting. Then there was the reckless killing of Alex Pretti, initially met with false allegations (implying Pretti was guilty of "domestic terrorism"), followed by a secret and delayed investigation.

According to a February 2026 study by the National Association of Criminal Defense Lawyers, the Justice Department secured an indictment in less than 11 percent of its prosecutions, a testament to the reckless disregard Trump's DOJ has for making and pursuing baseless charges.

> *The MAGA movement is a radical movement. . . . It is against the law of the United States and anti-rule-of-law in the United States.*
>
> —Circuit Judge J. Michael Luttig (ret.) (August 5, 2025)

IT was astonishing that a conservative jurist, once the darling of the Federalist Society and a favored choice for a Supreme Court seat, would be so outspoken, so dangerously anti-MAGA. It startled many in that conservative group. True, they had MAGA allegiance, but only up to a point. Still, silence was their craven option. As Peter Canellos of *Politico* put it in his 2026 book on the conservative legal movement:

> For active judges and justices who owed their careers to the conservative legal movement, the question was this: Would they feel free to stand against the person who enabled their success, thus showing that their movement was greater than politics? Or had the intense

> partisanship of the Trump era so altered their internal feedback loops that they could not see beyond the us-and-them of recent decades?

In the era of Trump 2.0, no perversion of the law is too great, whether hidden or open. By way of yet another example, Trump's Justice Department took brazen actions in April 2026. The plan was to push a far-fetched conspiracy theory in two ways: first, to prosecute those involved in the investigation into Russia and its potential ties to the 2016 Trump campaign; and second, to attempt to prosecute those overseeing the indictments related to the classified documents and Trump's attempt to overturn the 2020 presidential election. According to an April 19, 2026, *New York Times* report, the politically charged tactics used were Kafkaesque:

1. The senior federal prosecutor in Miami, who was to oversee the investigation, was removed.
2. Joseph diGenova, a former Trump lawyer, was named counselor to the attorney general and tasked with helping to prosecute the case.
3. The conspiracy case was to be brought before a grand jury in Fort Pierce, Florida,

which falls under the sole jurisdiction of federal judge Aileen M. Cannon, who issued favorable rulings for Trump in the classified documents case against him. For that, Trump praised her as "strong" and "brilliant."

4. One of the lawyers assigned to the case, Christopher-James DeLorenz, served as Judge Cannon's law clerk during the documents litigation.
5. Moreover, as reported in the *New York Times*, the posture of the case allows "the Justice Department to scrutinize in a single case matters that would normally be barred by the five-year statute of limitations. It would also give Mr. diGenova and Mr. Reding Quiñones [a Trump loyalist overseeing the case] the authority to scrutinize events that took place in Washington from their jurisdiction in Florida."
6. Again, according to the *Times*: "The Justice Department has also given Mr. Reding Quiñones special authority under a statute known as Section 515, the official said. That would enable him to bring indictments in jurisdictions where he is not the U.S. attorney."

Such actions typify the lengths to which Trump's compliant Justice Department will go to carry out his commands to persecute his political enemies and punish those who would dare to hold him accountable. Sadly, no action, however brazenly corrupt, unconstitutional, or fundamentally unjust, is beyond the pale for his willing henchmen.

Attacking Civil Rights and Racial Justice

In January 2018, Trump was emphatic when he spoke to reporters in Florida: "No, no, I'm not a racist. I am the least racist person you have ever interviewed." He has since echoed those words on numerous occasions.

His words were exposed for the outright lies they are with journalistic rigor and detailed documentation by Rachel Maddow on her May 4, 2026, MSNow program. In sum, she declared, what we have witnessed "since day one" of his second term is "a concerted and intense targeting of Black Americans, specifically, by this president and this administration."

The incriminating evidence is abundant. In 2018 he complained about immigrants from "shithole countries"—nations that are predominantly Black. A PBS news headline from October 30, 2025, revealed his white supremacist intent: "Trump limits annual

U.S. refugees to 7,500. It'll be mostly white South Africans."

In the early days of his administration, he issued executive orders to dismantle DEI programs across law firms, colleges, and other institutions. He then targeted affirmative action programs. Consistent with that, in September 2025, his solicitor general urged the U.S. Supreme Court to strike down state laws that redistricted congressional districts that sought to ensure fair representation for minority communities. In *Louisiana v. Callais* (2026), the conservative high court, with ample support from Trump's three appointees, granted that request, rendering a key provision of the 1965 Voting Rights Act that prohibits discrimination in voting "all but a dead letter," in Justice Elena Kagan's words.

Then there is this: Trump has fired Charles Q. Brown Jr. (chairman of the Joint Chiefs of Staff), Carla Hayden (Librarian of Congress), Gwynne Wilcox (National Labor Relations Board), Robert Primus (Surface Transportation Board), Alvin Brown (National Transportation Safety Board), Peggy Caar (National Center for Education Statistics), Willie Phillips (Federal Energy Regulatory Commission), Lisa Cook (Federal Reserve Board of Governors), and on and on. All of them are Black. As the *New*

York Times put it in a March 1, 2026, headline to a story by Erica L. Green: "Trump Says He Is the 'Least Racist' President. But His Term Echoes a Grim Past." That past dates back to the blatantly racist bent of the Wilson administration.

As Maddow noted, Trump rescinded Executive Order 11246 (sec. 202), first signed by Lyndon Johnson in 1965. The order prohibited federal contractors from discriminating "against any employee or applicant for employment because of race, color, religion, sex, sexual orientation, gender identity, or national origin." He also voided clause 52.222-21 of the Federal Acquisition Regulations, which prohibited segregated facilities.

During a 2024 interview with the National Association of Black Journalists in Chicago, Trump proclaimed: "I love the Black population of this country." Nothing could be further from the truth. His past and present actions make this abundantly clear.

Pleasing King Trump

Trump's firings of his secretary of Homeland Security, Kristi Noem, and his attorney general, Pam Bondi, reveal much about his mindset and what it takes to boost his ego. Despite her sycophantic demeanor, Noem's sin was that she upstaged her master in a self-serving, government-funded, $220 million ad campaign featuring herself decked in cowgirl gear and riding a horse. As cartoonish as it was, it put her in the limelight, which is reserved for her boss. That was unforgivable. Bondi's failing was of a different order. Her obsequious manner was insufficient to satisfy her boss. She couldn't deliver the kind of political retribution and prosecutorial revenge that Trump demanded. Even worse, she was unable to get the Jeffrey Epstein document scandal out of the news. The longer that shocking story stayed in the headlines, the more vulnerable Trump became. That, too, was unforgivable. Within a month's time, both women were forced out of their offices.

Had Noem and Bondi been more macho, more like "secretary of war" Pete Hegseth, they might have survived. True, he was also sycophantic, but he was much more than that. He was bold, decisive, unrelenting, reckless, and willing to break any legal or ethical norm to please Trump, whether it was committing alleged war crimes or ridding the military of all its female and minority leadership. Whatever it took, Pete got the job done.

Whatever the issue, the executive imperative was that the *king* was the law and never the other way around.

ICE Training: Ignore the Constitution

Part and parcel of the demand to ignore the laws of the land was the federal government's refusal to train its agents in the relevant laws governing their actions. For example, when a Homeland Security official testified before Congress in 2026, he revealed that for several months he watched "ICE dismantle the training program. Cutting 240 hours of vital classes from a 584-hour program—classes that teach the Constitution, our legal system, firearms training, the use of force, lawful arrests, proper detention, and the limits of officers' authority." He added: "New cadets are graduating from the academy despite widespread concerns among training staff that even in the final days of training, the cadets cannot demonstrate a solid grasp of the tactics or the law required to perform their jobs."

According to a *New York Times* report on February 23, 2026, such "disclosures underscore concerns about the conduct and preparedness of Homeland Security Department agents, who have shot and killed at least three American citizens over the last year. [Trump's] decision to order immigration officers into major American cities has led to a rise in violent encounters with members of the public, leading to fears that poor training for new agents will produce more chaos."

One shocking, but perhaps unsurprising, result of ICE's mass detentions, according to a May 13, 2026, *Politico* report, has been that "more than 10,000 times, judges have said those detentions, typically carried out with no opportunity for detainees to plead their case, were illegal. That's roughly 90 percent of all cases." This unprecedented rebuke from the federal judiciary speaks to the lawlessness of the Trump administration's immigration policies, which have shattered countless lives—not only the people targeted by ICE agents, many of whom have turned out to be in the country legally, including some U.S. citizens, but their spouses and children as well.

CONSTITUTIONAL government is much more than what is printed on parchment. Its ideals become real when *we the people* demand that the president and his officers respect the oath to faithfully "preserve, protect, and defend the Constitution."

IV

THOUGHTS ON LIBERTY

A constitution, as important as it is, will mean nothing unless the people are yearning for liberty and freedom.

—Ruth Bader Ginsburg (2012)

LIBERTY cannot thrive in the shadow of lies. To be truly free, a self-governing people need their government to be honest. Lies only benefit the ruler, not the ruled. Paine understood this, which is why he condemned "a willful, audacious libel against the truth [and] the common, good . . ." He noted that the problem worsens whenever lies are met with the kind of "silence" that encourages "base and wicked performances [that deserve] a general [condemnation] both by Congress and the People."

Donald Trump's method of spreading falsehoods has been as steady as it has been daring. He begins with a lie and keeps adding to it. He floods the zone with a barrage of new falsehoods. When confronted, he either denies having lied or viciously attacks the person exposing the lie. He hides one lie by uttering more lies on different topics. In the deceptive process, an Orwellian state of affairs becomes normal as the truth becomes abnormal, or is offered up as an executive entitlement. Truth, after all, is the prerogative of the powerful. It has no meaning in fact unless the facts serve the king's purpose. The king can do no wrong. If the king says it—to paraphrase disgraced former president Richard M. Nixon—it's not a lie. Only his adversaries lie—and they must be punished for their attacks on what the king has ordained to be true.

The War on American Values

American values and civility are under siege in the age of Trump. Truth loses its worth; compassion is debased; integrity is corrupted; unjust wars are justified; self-dealing is shamelessly practiced; electoral fairness is degraded; malice and revenge are normalized; lawlessness masquerades as justice; and respect for religious values is more a contrived shell game than a genuine article of faith.

There is no political or religious norm this president will not flout with contemptuous abandon. Whether it be portrayals of himself as the Savior, vile attacks on the pope (among others), despicable and unwarranted attacks on the recently deceased, nods to blatant racism, insane claims of false facts, or the strong-arm manipulation of his cabinet secretaries and the agencies they oversee, Trump has time and again proven himself to be an autocrat without equal in American history.

Gone are the faith of Washington, the promise of Jefferson, the genius of Madison, the dedication of Lincoln, the greatness of FDR, the vision of Reagan, and the hope of Obama.

In his delusional world, he stands *alone*; no one, dead or alive, can rival his supposed abilities and accomplishments. So great are his purported talents that monuments of all kinds must be erected in his honor, albeit at his punitive command.

The America of Abigail Adams, Sojourner Truth, Walt Whitman, Frederick Douglass, W.E.B. Du Bois, Louis Brandeis, Martin Luther King Jr., Earl Warren, and Harvey Milk is not his America—he has contempt for them. Rather, he hails the grifters, the charlatans, the authoritarians . . . but only so long as they bow to his authority. And by trickery and brashness, he has fooled his followers and persecuted his critics.

This is not the America of our ideals and our ancestors' hopes. Liberty is diminished each time Trump tightens the screws in his quest for yet more unbridled power. Our Republic is under siege. True patriots must oppose that curse with collective courage.

A Unique Danger

> *I cannot recall anything like this. I've been defending First Amendment rights since 2006, and this is the most serious of threats I can recall.*
>
> —Will Creeley
> (First Amendment lawyer)

It is common sense: to suppress free speech is to invite tyranny. To step forward, to speak out, to print freely, and to assemble and petition—those are the vital freedoms handed down to us by our founders. It is those freedoms, among others, that Trump and his cohort have abridged with deliberate abandon.

In the 250th year of our independence, he has further inflated his vanity in ways heretofore unheard of in our democratic republic. And while he has constantly exaggerated his worth, he has suppressed the views of those who refuse to bend the knee in his honor. To be his critic is to be an "enemy of the state." That is his mindset; that is his directive; and that has become the new normal in this age of Trump.

In both direct and indirect ways, he has tried to turn truth into falsehoods and vice versa. He has corrupted the truth to boost his power and divide the nation. In this tyrannical process, he has organized campaigns to scare anyone who doesn't follow his authoritarian message. Whether through bogus civil lawsuits or government overreach, the goal remains the same: to suppress opposing views.

His goal mocks the Madisonian aim of free speech for a free people, of that right to speak truth to tyranny, and to do so without fear of retaliation. Truth dies on such altars. By his suppressive measure, any truth that upsets him is branded as "fake." Faithful to his directives, his cabinet officials and his supplicants echo his false claims with vindictive vigor.

His strategy is as simple as it is malicious. Falsely attack his opponents and then commence severe punitive actions against them. Never mind whether such actions are warranted, lawful, or likely to be upheld by courts. The objective is fourfold:

> *First*—The aim is to punish his critics by attacking their reputations and then by forcing them to defend themselves, which can be burdensome and

costly. The aim is punitive, which is realized even in the absence of a judicial victory.

Second—The larger objective is to chill the speech of others who might dare to disobey his ideological and self-serving edicts. If anyone ventures to challenge him, they too can expect to be criminally charged, arrested, fined, civilly sued, or investigated by his enforcers ad infinitum. By that suppressive logic, even if he loses one case or another, he can nonetheless claim victory by chilling the expression of countless others who fear getting in his crosshairs.

Third—Here, the punitive focus is on members of the press who refuse to produce reports that please the president and his underlings. As a result, the Pentagon imposed restrictions on news outlets, threatening to revoke their press passes for any critical reporting. In March 2026, a federal court ruled that the Pentagon's policy favored reporters who were "willing to publish only stories that are favorable to or spoon-fed by department leadership." That ruling followed a similarly strict decision by a federal judge who ruled that the administration had to restore the operations of Voice of America after Trump's executive order attempted to shut it down. True to such brazen abridgments of the First Amendment, Defense Secretary Pete Hegseth barred press photographers who dared to post "unflattering" photos of the secretary.

Fourth—Beyond such unconstitutional measures, Federal Communications Commission Chairman Brendan Carr is quick to threaten reporters and news outlets with regulatory punishments if they disparage the president and his underlings. To bolster his bravado, he has also threatened to block media mergers if the parent stations refused to honor Trump's will.

To be sure, many of these actions violate the First Amendment, as well as basic notions of fairness. But so what? Trump doesn't care. If the minions in his cabinet, Congress, or on the courts cannot satisfy his particular wishes, he resorts to fear, which is his main tactic.

Time and again, he has abused his constitutional authority by persecuting those who refuse to toe his line, including law firms, universities, media outlets, libraries, museums, students, and former and current government officials.

The result: *we the people* must forfeit our rights for fear of being punished for peacefully exercising them. The president approves; his attorney general applauds;

his FBI director cheers; as do all those other cabinet secretaries and administration officials—flunkies who do his bidding. His will, however unhinged, is their marching orders. Simply consider the following five examples, among numerous others:

The evidence of this refusal to honor his constitutional oath is abundant. For example:

1. Trump has ordered his administration to retaliate against law firms whose lawyers have been critical of him or opposed his false-election claims (Executive Order No. 14230). As a federal district court judge put it in *Perkins Coie LLP v. U.S. Dept. of Justice* (2025): "No American President has ever before issued executive orders like the one at issue targeting a prominent law firm with adverse actions. . . . The instant case presents an unprecedented attack on . . . the foundational principles" of the Constitution and Bill of Rights. Three hundred and four days later, the Justice Department dropped its legal defense of the president's executive orders punishing the four firms. "It offered no explanation to either the parties or the court for its reversal. We remain committed to defending our firm, our people, and our

clients." But "hours after asking the court to dismiss its appeal, the Department of Justice . . . abruptly reversed course and moved to continue its defense of the unconstitutional executive orders," Perkins Coie said in a statement immediately thereafter.

2. On February 14, 2025, Trump's then-acting assistant secretary for civil rights went after law firms, libraries, colleges, and others to eradicate diversity, equity, and inclusion (DEI) programs, in the absence of basic due process definitions of the behavior being regulated. The government "guidelines" were so unconstitutionally vague that "even the Government does not know what constitutes DEI-regulated speech that violates federal anti-discrimination laws" (*National Association of Diversity Officers v. Donald Trump* [D.M., 2025]).
3. Trump has defamed and threatened those in the press who refuse to kowtow to his creed and who speak ill of him, either by way of news reports or comical satires. In one of his social media posts, he labeled the media outlets and reporters who opposed his views as "the ENEMY OF THE PEOPLE!"

4. Either by way of a personal lawsuit for alleged defamation or FCC regulatory threats (e.g., the FCC's threatened licensing revocation actions against CBS's *60 Minutes* and its attacks on the late-night host Jimmy Kimmel), he has used his powers to chill the speech of anyone who dares to condemn him. Such retaliatory attacks include a $10 billion defamation lawsuit against the *Wall Street Journal* and a $1.1 billion cut in public broadcasting funds to NPR and PBS stations. In 2024, he even sued the *Des Moines Register* and Iowa pollster Ann Selzer over a poll that predicted former Vice President Kamala Harris would win the presidential election. Furthermore, after the U.S.-based artificial intelligence (AI) company Anthropic refused to allow its services to be used for mass domestic surveillance of Americans, he ordered all federal agencies to stop using the company. His "secretary of war" then designated Anthropic as a "supply-chain risk to national security," which meant that no contractor that works with the military could do business with the company.

5. He has quite often unlawfully asserted his ideological biases to go after museums, parks, and libraries whose expression is contrary to his views of how America's history is to be portrayed. This governmental attack on the free flow of information undermines fundamental American values.

In case after case, he has used patently unlawful methods (wildly violative of basic due process norms) to chill the speech of those persecuted as well as those countless other bystanders who could face a similar fate. And time and again, he has exceeded his constitutional authority in violation of powers entrusted to Congress—also in violation of the First Amendment. And yet a subservient and timid Republican majority of the House and Senate has succumbed to his imperious will.

Finally, mountains of government information have either been destroyed or removed from public access. Though not a technical First Amendment violation, such destruction and suppression of information runs contrary to the norms of the Freedom of Information Act and the spirit of the First Amendment.

The Practice of Pretense

There is also the hypocrisy so much at play here. Consider, for example, what he promised on the occasion of his second inaugural address on January 20, 2025:

> After years and years of illegal and unconstitutional federal efforts to restrict free expression, I will also sign an executive order to immediately stop all government censorship and bring back free speech to America.

Then, in his executive order on the same day, the new president issued an order titled "Restoring Freedom of Speech and Ending Federal Censorship." In it, he declared, "Government censorship of speech is intolerable in a free society." Let no one forget what his then–designate attorney general Pam Bondi pledged during her confirmation hearing: "Under my watch, the partisan weaponization of the Department of Justice will end. America must have one tier of justice for all."

Know this: it is not partisan to expose and denounce the actions of a president and his administration whenever they abridge our free expression rights. In that respect, Trump is no more or less deserving of condemnation than oppressive executive actions taken by figures like John Adams (the Alien and Sedition Acts) and Woodrow Wilson (the Espionage Act of 1917 and the Sedition Act of 1918). Even so, and unlike the case with Trump, both Adams and Wilson at least sought congressional approval for their suppressive actions.

Inform yourself. Think critically. Stand up. Speak out. And finally, heed what Justice Hugo Black exhorted in his inspiring dissent in *In re Anastaplo* (1961): "We must not be afraid to be free." Likewise, we must not be afraid to let *others* be free. With Trump and his confederates, freedom is only the prerogative of those who obey his will, which is an Orwellian form of freedom.

V

TO SECURE THE BLESSINGS OF LIBERTY AND EQUALITY

The secret of liberty is always, in the end, the courage to resist.

—Harold Laski (1949)

FREEDOM of speech, press, and assembly, along with the right to protest, are vital to liberty in our constitutional democracy. Violating or restricting these rights is an invitation to tyranny. These fundamental rights have been abridged too frequently and in severe ways. They have also been violated in the name of political retribution. This is an old problem that the founders addressed, initially through expressive means and later through constitutional measures.

ON August 14, 1765, in Boston, enraged colonists gathered around the effigy of a man hanging from a branch of an old oak tree. On Orange Street, near the commons, the Loyal Nine (activist merchants and artisans) assembled to protest the Stamp Act and the local resident, Andrew Oliver, who collected the taxes. As Stephen Solomon notes in his book *Revolutionary Dissent*, when "word of the spectacle spread throughout the city, hundreds of people gathered around the tree." People gathered, talked, exchanged ideas, and yes, protested. The seeds of dissent had already been stirring in the soil; it symbolized an American spirit that would, in time, help create a government based on liberty. And all of this happened a quarter of a century before the ratification of the First Amendment.

There is a lesson here: silent obedience invites tyranny, while active engagement challenges it. Perfunctory acquiescence—which has afflicted so many—is contrary to the kind of constitutional government handed down to us. The 1765 patriots of Boston understood that if despotism went unchallenged, if kingly power remained unchecked, and if citizens stayed uninvolved, then the future of democracy was doomed.

What *We the People* Can Do

What, then, should you do? Think and act in the spirit of Paine, Jefferson, and figures like Frederick Douglass, Dr. Martin Luther King, Elizabeth Cady Stanton, and John Lewis. To start, align your thinking with things to avoid. For instance, don't let the status quo become normal; don't let falsehoods go unchallenged; don't allow our history to be distorted for self-serving and divisive goals; don't remain passive in the face of oppression; don't be intimidated by bullies; don't ignore the evils of brutality; don't tolerate government censorship in schools, libraries, media, or elsewhere; don't retreat from defending liberty and equality; don't confuse love of country with love of political party; and don't lose faith in our American ideals.

By the same token, and as Paine wrote in 1783, to "pass from the extremes of danger to safety"—from the tumult of oppression to the tranquility of freedom—we urge resolute use of our First Amendment freedoms. Those freedoms, after all, were designed to encourage dissent, safeguard against government abuse, and allow people to act according to their own consciences. In this, the 250th year of our independence, Timothy Snyder, author of *On Tyranny*, reminds us that for "authoritarians to win, they need their supporters to be active, the majority to be silent, and their actions to seem normal. Protest shows that their supporters are in the minority, that the majority will not be silent, and that it is the people who set the standards. Protest summons more protest. When some of us act, others will follow."

Effective dissent requires dispassionate thinking and creative alternatives. Here are eight suggestions:

1. **Identify the problem:** Explain and document the nature and scope of the problem.
2. **Take collective action:** There is safety in numbers. When individuals, law firms, or colleges stand alone, they are most vulnerable.
3. **Don't settle for mass one-day, feel-good demonstrations:** Peaceful dissent is important, but it must be linked with other actions as *creatively* and *continually* as possible.
4. **Take targeted messages and organizing to all states:** Educate and inform residents in red and blue states how economic and other harms affect them.
5. **Create a united front:** We cannot afford to be siloed. We need cross-communication and cross-action—e.g., civil rights groups

working with other groups, along with law firms and civic groups, etc.

6. **Develop a "big tent" approach to action:** Lawyers must join with educators, writers, artists, politicians, religious leaders, and activists to combat authoritarianism.
7. **Flood the zone with daily actions and press coverage:** Counter the momentum of Trump's repetition of lies with facts, truth, and examples.
8. **Insist that concerned lawmakers voice effective strategies for united action.**

Protesting requires standing up, speaking out, and joining others. Even though no one will pay you to do this (despite Trump's false claims to the contrary), participating in peaceful protests helps build community, overcomes feelings of helplessness, and sends a clear message to supporters (including those who can't attend), the opposition, and those who are too cynical, apathetic, or hopeless to join. Images of millions of Americans across the country—not just in big cities but also in small towns in every state, from Idaho to Alabama—protesting this administration's actions with good humor and without violence, show not only our numbers but also our strength.

They remind the government that the tradition of self-determination in democracy is alive and well. So, stand up! Be peaceful, but stay resolute. Here are 10 suggestions:

1. **Participate in "No Kings" protests.** Bring your family and friends. Bring signs, sing songs, display placards, and peacefully assemble in public spaces. Encourage as diverse a group as possible.
2. **Protest in front of places where your presence can be seen and your grievances heard.** Protest where your voice can be felt. Protest at locations where tyranny is either perpetuated or defended. For example, peacefully gather and protest in front of the Federal Communications Commission (FCC) to let its chairman, Brendan Carr, and local television and radio stations, know that you oppose his suppression of freedom of the press; or protest near the Department of Justice to make clear to the current attorney general that you detest their politicization of the law. Do the same for other local federal government buildings and courthouses outside of Washington, D.C.,

where tyranny is practiced. The same might be said for peaceful protests in front of the Supreme Court whenever it continues to shamelessly justify authoritarianism.

3. **Protest outside businesses that support tyranny.** For example, peacefully gather and demonstrate in front of media outlets that consistently back Trump's tyranny.
4. **Defend those under attack.** For example, if a law firm is under a government attack, gather around to show your support for standing up to Trumpian bullies.
5. **Join counterprotests.** If a group like Moms for Liberty demands book bans at libraries, attend local council meetings to oppose the suppression of ideas. Support libraries that oppose book bans.
6. **Use every form of media,** e.g., TikTok, Instagram, X (Twitter), Facebook, YouTube, Blue Sky, Threads, Mastodon, and national and local newspapers, radio, and TV to oppose Trump's unlawful and immoral practices. Issue press releases, pitch news stories, and write letters to the editor.
7. **Be creative in protesting.** For example, pool your money with others to buy targeted

billboards with "no kings" messages and similar ideas. Or use art and/or music to make your oppositional point.

8. **Put Trump politics on the agendas of your political, religious, or social group** to express your concerns about the future of our republic.
9. **Run for elective office.** Raise the voice of your community.
10. **And VOTE!** Show up for all elections (primary, general, school board, local, state, and national) and vote to end tyranny.

And let us not forget that liberty only exists when it is actively maintained. It diminishes when taken for granted. Our founders, imperfect as they were, wisely designed a Constitution that could be amended to adapt as humanity progressed. Over 250 years, the United States has gradually, though unevenly, moved toward greater liberty—for enslaved people, people of color, women, Native Americans, poor people, LGBTQ+ individuals and families, immigrants, religious minorities, and other dissenters—despite fierce opposition from those who wish to restrict the freedoms of others. Today, there are those who would dismantle our democracy to ensure that only a select few are truly free. To safeguard liberty, we must:

- Remember our past, but only in honest ways.
- Remember the sacrifices made on our behalf by those who struggled in its name.
- Remember that scapegoating the innocent, deeming those who are different or who dissent as "the enemy within," is never justifiable.
- Remember that patriotism must be rooted in *our* ideals and not in knee-jerk obedience to the dictates of the powerful.
- Remember, democracies don't survive on their own; they need faithful and perpetual support.
- Remember, our Republic needs *we the people* to stand up.

The Threat of Despotism

The well-being of democracy is what we make it, but only if we make it wisely. It is the "madness of folly" to expect justice from despots; it is dangerous to believe that our democracy will not perish when attacked by authoritarianism. It is a catastrophic mistake, as Timothy Snyder has warned, "to assume that rulers who came to power through institutions cannot change or destroy those very institutions—even when that is exactly what they have announced that they will do."

We the people cannot afford to make such mistakes. To believe otherwise is perilous. The politics of denial leads to a politics of suppression. Hence, the wrongs of the present will live on to produce the evils of the future. If our time "is out of joint," then we must join together "to set it right." That is more than a Shakespearean insight; it is the sacred duty of all who hold that "governments derive their power from the consent of the governed and that people have the right to alter or abolish destructive governments." To abolish oppression is not to abolish our constitutional system; rather, it is to reinvigorate it, to give it an infusion of new life.

From Pennsylvania Avenue in Washington, D.C., to Nicollet Avenue in Minneapolis, the politics of the powerful has been built on lies compounded by a toxic faith in the goodness of an all-powerful ruler. That danger is spreading across America like a wildfire set ablaze by a madman, a greedy man, a vengeful man, and a man whose allegiance is grounded in his vanity—not our *Declaration*, not our *Constitution*, and not our *laws*.

Trump's vanity and bluster know no bounds; he shows no respect for checks and balances; he lies habitually; he disregards the rule of law; he demonizes anyone who opposes him; and he finds comfort in others' misery. This would-be despot and the movement he leads pose a clear and immediate danger to our system of constitutional democracy.

Toward "a More Perfect Union"

On September 18, 1787, the last day of the Constitutional Convention, Elizabeth Willing Powel asked Benjamin Franklin whether the nation would have a monarchy or a republic. He responded, "A republic, if you can keep it." Those cautionary words were spoken before the U.S. Constitution was ratified, along with its preamble that aimed for "a more perfect Union." In other words, the blood of revolutionary patriots had to be followed by the will of subsequent generations to preserve and perfect the ideals of our founders. In *Erasing History* (2026 ed.), Jason Stanley wisely advises that "the restoration of history is crucial to the defense of democracy." To move forward, we must honestly reflect on the past and accept both its good and bad aspects, even if it makes us uncomfortable. Lies may make some feel better, but they don't make us better.

Reflect on all of this, take action, and strive to make our America "a more perfect Union." For there is no everlasting guarantee that a great nation and its cherished values will survive. Many governments, including venerable ones, have fallen over time. Freedom must be sustained through sacrifice. When it is deprived, what remains is the pain caused by the loss of liberty and equality. Tyranny leads to hopelessness unless it is challenged with the strength befitting a free people.

"We are living in a time when it is hard to hope," as former president Barack Obama said at the funeral of civil rights leader Jesse Jackson in March 2026. Still, in an era of fear and despair, we refuse to be afraid or lose faith in our system of constitutional government. We refuse to bow to the will of authoritarians.

We four Delawareans respectfully present to you, our fellow Americans, our concerns and advice in the hope that the America Paine envisioned and Jefferson inspired 250 years ago will help us all better secure the blessings of true liberty and equality. Join us and reaffirm our cherished American principles before it's too late.

"A REPUBLIC, IF YOU CAN KEEP IT."
This response, attributed to Benjamin Franklin as he left the Constitutional Convention on September 17, 1787, was offered in reply to Elizabeth Willing Powel, who asked, "Well, Doctor, what have we got, a republic or a monarchy?" His famous reply warns that our republic's continuing survival depends on the active, informed involvement of its citizens.

ACTIVISTS' RESOURCES

WHAT follows is a select list of books to inform, inspire, and motivate you on how best to think about current threats to our democracy. A QR code that links to our website, Common Sense USA, is also included to help readers identify peaceful actions they might take to oppose tyranny.

Publications

Angwin, Julia, and Ami Fields-Meyer. *On Courage: How to Be a Dissident in an Age of Fear*. Mariner Books, 2026.

Applebaum, Anne. *Autocracy, Inc.: The Dictators Who Want to Run the World*. Doubleday, 2024.

Applebaum, Anne. *Twilight of Democracy: The Seductive Lure of Authoritarianism*. Vintage, 2021.

Arendt, Hannah. *On Lying and Politics*. Introduction by David Bromwich. Library of America, 2022.

Arendt, Hannah. *The Origins of Totalitarianism*. Introduction by Anne Applebaum. Mariner Books, 2024.

Arendt, Hannah, and Henry David Thoreau. *On Civil Disobedience*. Edited by Roger Berkowitz. Library of America, 2024.

Browne-Marshall, Gloria J. *A Protest History of the United States*. Beacon Press, 2025.

Ferlinghetti, Lawrence. *Poetry as Insurgent Art*. New Directions, 1975.

Gregor, Neil. *How to Read Hitler*. Norton, 2005.

Griffith, Elizabeth. *Formidable: American Women and the Fight for Equality: 1920–2020*. Pegasus Books, 2022.

King, Martin Luther Jr. *Letter from Birmingham Jail*. Penguin Classics, 2018.

King, Martin Luther Jr. *Stride Toward Freedom: The Montgomery Story*. Edited by Clayborne Carson. Beacon Press, 2010.

King, Martin Luther Jr. *Where Do We Go from Here: Chaos or Community?* Beacon Press, 2010.

King, Martin Luther Jr. *Why We Can't Wait*. Signet, 2000.

Larson, Eric. *Declaring Independence: Why 1776 Matters*. W.W. Norton, 2025.

Lewis, John, and Michael D'Orso. *Walking with the Wind: A Memoir of the Movement*. Simon & Schuster, 2015.

Maddow, Rachel. *Prequel: An American Fight Against Fascism*. Crown, 2023.

Meacham, Jon, ed. *American Struggle: Democracy, Dissent, and the Pursuit of a More Perfect Union: An Anthology*. Random House, 2026.

Meacham, Jon. *His Truth Is Marching On: John Lewis and the Power of Hope*. Random House, 2020.

Paine, Thomas. *Collected Writings*. Edited by Eric Foner. Library of America, 1995.

Parkinson, Robert G. *Tyrants and Rogues: Understanding the Declaration of Independence*. W.W. Norton, 2026.

Raskin, Jamie. *Unthinkable: Trauma, Truth, and the Trials of American Democracy*. Harper, 2022.

Rosen, Jeffrey. *The Pursuit of Liberty: How Hamilton vs. Jefferson Ignited the Lasting Battle over Power in America*. Simon & Schuster, 2025.

Shaw, Randy. *The Activist's Handbook: A Primer*. University of California Press, 2013.

Snyder, Timothy. *On Freedom*. Crown Publishing, 2024.

Snyder, Timothy. *On Tyranny: Twenty Lessons from the Twentieth Century*. Crown Publishing, 2016.

Solomon, Stephen. *Revolutionary Dissent: How the Founding Generation Created Freedom of Speech*. St. Martin's Press, 2016.

Stanley, Jason. *Erasing History: How Fascists Rewrite the Past to Control the Future*. One Signal Publishers/ Atria, 2026.

Stanley, Jason. *How Fascism Works: The Politics of Us and Them*. Random House, 2020.

Stanley, Jason. *How Propaganda Works*. Princeton University Press, 2016.

Online Resources

American Civil Liberties Union (ACLU). Defends civil liberties and civil rights. https://www.aclu.org.

Democracy Now! Producer of a daily, global, independent news hour hosted by award-winning journalists Amy Goodman and Juan González. https://www.democracynow.org.

Indivisible. A national, on-the-ground, volunteer-led group opposed to abuses of government power, working with local communities. https://indivisible.org.

Martyrs Day. A call to remember the protesters who have given their lives in the struggle for justice, annually on July 5. https://martyrsday.us.

We Hold These Truths. Unites people across the political spectrum, promoting civic values that are increasingly under threat. https://weholdtruths.org.

Common Sense USA

commonsense-usa.com

ABOUT THE AUTHORS

RONALD K.L. COLLINS is a retired law professor and author or coauthor of 13 books. He was a law clerk to Oregon Supreme Court Justice Hans Linde and thereafter served as a Supreme Court fellow to Chief Justice Warren Burger. He is the Lewes Public Library's Distinguished Lecturer and cofounder of the History Book Festival.

RUSSELL W. HUXTABLE is a Delaware state senator and former nonprofit leader. His work has focused on affordable housing, capacity building, and expanding opportunities so communities can thrive. He sees democracy as a shared responsibility.

AMY L. MARASCO is an accomplished public servant who builds consensus and common-sense solutions for her constituents. She served on the town council and was vice mayor of a rural Virginia community, and now serves as the mayor of Lewes, Delaware, the first town in the first state. She is the coauthor (with Ronald Collins) of "250 Years Ago, the Seeds of Dissent Stirred in Lewes," National Constitution Center website (August 20, 2025).

PAUL M. SPARROW is a writer and historical consultant; the former director of the Franklin D. Roosevelt Presidential Library and Museum; and a deputy director and senior vice president at the Newseum in Washington, D.C. He is an Emmy award–winning television producer and author of *Awakening the Spirit of America: FDR's War of Words with Charles Lindbergh* (2024).

www.ingramcontent.com/pod-product-compliance
Lightning Source LLC
LaVergne TN
LVHW051013080826
845145LV00009B/2601

* 9 7 8 1 9 3 8 9 3 8 8 3 2 *